Maybe They Were Right

The Adolescent Guide To A Better Future

Kas Arkbar

Author by Kas Arbar

Self-Published by Kas Arkbar

To contact the author:

Kas Arkbar

Email address: naucetheboss@gmail.com

Introduction

As the sun sets, another day comes to an end. Blessed to be alive, is what most would say! A lot of people did not wake up this morning. There are a lot of people that made plans that will never be fulfilled. What was your purpose? Why are we here? No one knows. We are all trying to figure this thing out and put the pieces back together. Make sense of this life if you will. No one's perfect but the best thing for anyone growing up is to have someone you can talk to. Someone you can learn from, relate to, and confide in. Unfortunately, a lot of people never get that luxury. We learn from experiences, mistakes, and life is tough with no guarantees. We all can use someone who can help us along this journey. A person that can fill in the blanks for most situations whether good or bad. Lend me your ears and eyes. Let me be that guide to help you become a better person. Are you ready?

Table of Contents

Chapter 1

Be A Kid

A lot of times when growing up, we always wish we did not have to listen to our parents. They think they know every damn thing, don't they? They tell us when to go to bed, when to wake up, what chores to do, how to dress, what to eat, what we can and can't do, what kind of grades to get, when to get off the phone, putting us on punishment, all types of crap! I mean geez mom I got this. I am a big kid, I'm a teenager, you are just an adult, you know nothing about the struggles us kids go through. Sometimes, you wish they would just butt out and let you live your damn life! Sounds like you right? I bet even sometimes you try to hang around adults and try to listen to their conversations to be a little nosey. I don't know about you but I got them curse words just so I could say it on the playground to show my friends I was cool and grown. Hey girl, get that mutha fuckin jump rope out of here! Wilson you keep playing with me and I'm going to break my foot off in your black ass! You know that type of shit.

Anyway, if you grew up in a black household like mine you might have heard get your ass out of here, stop trying to be so dam grown, mind your own business, stay in a child's place, or go play with them other kids before I whoop your ass. Yea, baby I remember all that shit. Hell, if it wasn't said to me, I heard it told to my cousins and if not that I heard other people I did not know tell their kids that at the park or the store. It was easy for your ass to get popped if she told you "don't go touching nothing when we get into the store and I don't have no damn money so don't be asking for shit". Or you might get that "boy don't embarrass me or you better act like you got some common sense and manners". Soon as you even looked like you were going to do something bad, you got that look of death. Hell, some of yawl might have got the one when they grab your arm tight as hell, squeeze it and say what did I tell your ass. Trust and believe it was none of that time out Timmy shit either and you better not cry, or they were going to give you something to cry about.

Once that "abuse" kicks in when you become of age, we all think soon as I get old enough, I am out of this mutha. She cannot be talking to me like this, dam all this! She always telling me what to do, always asking me to get the remote when it's right next to her bed, always asking me to get her some red Kool aid or Pepsi while I am playing my video games. Matter of fact, she is always telling me to wash the dishes, take the garbage out, ENOUGH IS ENOUGH!

I'm a kid, I got cartoons to watch, friends to talk to, jumping on the bed, things to do! Mom is tripping and my pops (if he is around) is acting up. I cannot wait to move out and be on my own. Ima have a car, my own place, a couple of bad chicks and so much money! I will be living it up! You've been there, right? Feeling just like me, right? But hold on playboy and hold that thought sister girl (NOTE TO SELF.... you got to tilt your head and snap your fingers when you say sister girl). Believe it or not, all this is just preparing you for the real world. In a weird way your parents, guardians or whoever decided to raise your ass is trying to instill some valuable lessons and quality life skills in your behind. They are trying to help; you just do not see it at this time. I assure you if your future self were able to contact you, they would say hey little ninja, enjoy your youth. Your parents are actually trying to help you. Enjoy your childhood, enjoy the fun you have with your friends before the real world of work and responsibility hit your ass with a stone-cold stunner (now give me a hell yea!).

Life moves faster than you think, and you are going to be older way longer than you are younger. I can guarantee you every adult sits and wish they could go back in time and just enjoy being a kid. When you are an adult, life is not easy as you think. It is difficult and trying a lot of times. The reality of it is a lot of times you may have to do a lot of things you will

9

not like. It is a lot of sacrificing, a lot of disappointments in people and choices we make. As a kid you have no idea of what lies ahead. You are trying to figure things out and at the same time your parents and other adults may be still trying to figure it out as well. Now, it is not a bad thing (actually, it is if you make the wrong decisions) but growing up is something we all must do. The point I am trying to express to you is just live in the moment, enjoy this time of less responsibility and youth because once it is gone it is gone forever. That is unless you were born into a rich family or you hit the lottery and if that is the case none of this shit applies to you.

Chapter 2

Don't Take Everything Personal

In life man, it is easy to get into your feelings. People may say things to you that might hurt you, make you feel some type of way, reject you, disagree with you, turn you down but you can't take it personal. You must scoop up the broken pieces inside of you, wipe them tears away, remove that doubt, and keep on moving. Now, I am not saying it's going to be easy playboy, it's difficult as hell sometimes but you've got to keep pushing. This will save you a lot of time and energy trust me.

Perfect example, I remember when I was in the 3rd grade there was a little light brown skin cutie in my class, and I had the biggest crush on her. My mom used to give me a couple of dollars for allowance, so I decided I'll show this girl how much I like her. Now, some of yawl might not know what working for allowance is but yea ninja, I had to wash dishes, sweep the floors, clean my room, watch star search (you probably don't even know what star search is but so what!) all that! My mom was not just flat out giving me money I had to earn it! But anyway. I went into this punk ass corner store across the street from the school and I saw these hoop earrings. I say to myself "hey if I get these earrings boomsheeka going to be feeling the kid" (NOTE TO SELF: her name wasn't actually boomsheeka but I can't think of her name right now... besides it was 3rd grade ninja how am I supposed to remember that). Anyway, I buy these cheap ass earrings and give it to her on the playground and she goes "Aww thank you" and walks away. I am like "yeaaa, I'm in the door now" but suddenly, she starts talking to this boy named Corey all smiling up in this ninja face. Now, Corey was a pretty little light skin ninja all the girls liked and apparently boomsheeka liked his ass too! So here I am, already spent my little bit of money on her ass trying to profess my love and she is up in Corey's face. Damn, what could a ninja do! Now, with all this playing out like it did, you know I wanted to take my shit back from her ass, but I could not because PLAYGROUND RULES were in effect. Now PLAYGROUND RULES told me you cannot be an Indian giver or an African booty scratcher, so I had to take that loss. Needless to say, it did not work out with boomsheeka, yea I was hurt but the point was I couldn't take it personal. I liked her but she did not like me and according to a glass of cold milk that is the way the cookie crumbles sometimes.

12

Now, when you hold onto things for too long it really damages you. I know you might be thinking, "I can't believe this mutha clucka said this to me"! I cannot believe she left me or such and such did this to me! Unfortunately, things like this will happen and it is something you cannot control. As people, we must forgive whoever wronged us and keep pushing. Now, you may say "I'm not forgiving nobody"! You don't know what they said to me, you don't know how they hurt me, you don't know how my parents left me or wasn't there for me, but the forgiveness isn't for them it's for you. When you do not forgive, you are trapped in whatever moment in time that thing happened. Here you go mad at someone for what they did to you 10 years ago, but that person moved on with their life and they're not even thinking about what they did to you and in most cases (depending on the circumstances). You feel sick when you see them, tension binds up in your chest and stomach, you're mad and that person who sometimes has no clue or does not even remember what they did to you. They're out here living their best life and you're still mad as hell. Even if they apologize, you are not accepting it. Trust me man you've got to let it go! Once again, it is not for them it is for you. If you let go, you will save yourself a lot of time, stress, health, and mental issues.

Also, know that everyone does not have to agree with you and most people will not. Yes, they may not be on your level and vice versa but everyone is entitled to their own opinion whether right or wrong. People can have an intelligent debate. We can agree to disagree and that is what makes the world what it is, but you cannot be mad if they do not see your point. Just hearing a person out, I believe is the best thing. Some people will shut down when they feel you are coming at them sideways. Do not try to dominate the conversation just because you think your knowledge on a situation is more superior. No one can learn anything when arrogance is involved. When the table of dialogue is an even stream of communication, we all win.

Chapter 3

Life Isn't Easy

From the door, if you accept life is not fair and nobody owes you anything, you will be alright. Trust me playboy, the older you get you will eventually see how rigged the game truly is. Listen here, I am trying to tell you sister girl they are not playing fair out here in the real world or these internet streets. No matter how qualified you think you are, they will definitely show you (insert the late great James Brown's voice) it is a man's world, o excuse me, correction a white man's world just so you know. Life is so not fair, people who cheated the system have a super head start while the rest of us have to struggle and get the scraps that fall on the floor if you are lucky. Do you think most people and parents chose the job they are currently working at and it's what they wanted? Hell, to the nah, nah, nah. A lot of people did what they had to do to make ends meet. Student loans came knocking, babies were on the way, big momma needed help with the rent at home and they had to step up. Life will always throw you some bullshit so be ready to duck once in a while.

Also, keep in mind no one is willing to give you anything for free unless you got the hook up my friend and even then, you are going to have to pay up somewhere down the line eventually. The hook up is one of the major keys to making it in the world if you ask me. Everything is all about who you know and not what you know. What you know will help you stay but who you know gets you in the door. Man listen, you have no idea how many people got jobs because their father knows this guy, or they were in this fraternity together, or such and such mom knows this person and they did a favor for yada, yada. It is an endless cycle of "hey my ninja I got you". That does not work for a lot of people but if you are fortunate enough to get a hook up who wouldn't take it? Hell, if I saw you in the line at the club or great adventures and you said hey ninja, want a ditch? You damn straight I am taking it! Besides who would want to go all the way to the back of the line, when my people hooking me up right? That is straight commonsense bro and that my friend is the magic of the hook up.

On the other end, for people with no chance of a hook up, you've got to work harder. Shit sometimes 10 times harder to get where you're trying to go. Hell, negro you've got to work hard for anything that you want in life. If you want something, you have to truly go after it despite what other people may think or tell you. For example, look at one of the greatest basketball players ever Michael Jordan. When he was in high school, no one was looking at him, he got cut from the team, they said he wasn't good enough, so what does he do? He worked harder, kept going after it. Jordan was so determined to prove people wrong despite what they all told him. He was not going to stop until he was right. Years later, he exceeded their expectations and did what they told him he could not do. On top of that this ninja threw it up in their faces at his hall of fame speech when it was all said and done. Man, this is your life and your dreams so follow your heart whether they believe in you or not. We all need to do what makes us happy ultimately because you do not want to be living someone else's dream. Also, keep in mind sometimes you still have to do what you got to do, even if you do not want to. And sometimes you've got to put your dreams on hold for a while but hey man that is the life of an adult.

Now, do not get me wrong people may have certain dreams or aspirations for you. They may feel they need to stop you from making the same mistakes they made and there is nothing wrong with that. Your parents may feel you are going to do what they say, go to college, get this job they want you to have and that is that. It is their job to protect you and all they are trying to do is set you up properly so you can live a good life with less problems than they had and yada, yada, yada. That is fine and dandy and that is what they are trying to do but when you become of age, you're going to be the one left living your life. The decisions you make going forward will affect how things turn out for you. Everyone makes good and bad choices but that's what life is about, but if you remember like I said life isn't fair or right, you will be more receptive or be less shocked when things happen but hey what do I know. A lot of people always get dealt a bad hand that did not deserve it and a lot of people always get breaks or get away with everything so that's just how things work, I guess. Hey man it's just my opinion you didn't ask for but once again I am trying to give you a couple of gems to make your journey and transition down this path a little easier. And that right there **sets the stage for me because if everyone viewed the world in the same light, they might be less disappointed. Plus, this should help you see the world for what it really is, politics and bullshit.**

Chapter 4

Take Advice

Always listen to what someone has to say even if you don't agree with them or see their point. What you need to understand is most people at some point were you and that is why they say the things they say. Most people can look at you and know what you're going through or about to go through. A lot of adults spend time reflecting on a lot of past decisions whether good or bad wishing they had a time machine so they can go back and change or undo certain situations and you know why? It's because someone in their youth tried to tell them and they did not listen and after everything that happened, they wished they did. So, what do some do? They try to help prevent you from making those mistakes and give you an insight to hopefully help you out, so you do not do what they did. You may even get others like myself giving you information to guide you to a better life to avoid certain pitfalls. But the problem is kids just do not listen. They think they know everything. A lot of kids do not have the mind or foresight to see what is going on or will be going on and it is not their fault. Most kids not all, but most kids are quick to dismiss what an adult is trying to tell them, and you know how I know? I did the same shit when I was younger, duh.

Here is an example, I remember I was in the 7th or 8th grade and my mother wanted to give me a Pea coat my uncle gave her to give to me and I didn't know what it was at the time. She goes, "boy you want this coat"? I looked at it and I am like "nope". She says "WHAT!" I am like "nope I don't like it". She goes "Boy this is a Pea coat you know! You sure you don't want this coat"? I am like "nope, I don't want it". She goes "Boy You Sure" I say "yep, I'm sure". She just shakes her head and says "alright". In my mind, I am like "get that ugly ass coat out of here". It wasn't a triple fat goose coat, goose down or duck down for that matter (you have no clue what those are but so what). If I wore that coat to school, I would be looking like a straight sucker... Now, lo and behold I go to school the next day and my classmates Chuck and Jameel are sitting there talking. As they are talking, I noticed Jameel has on the same coat my mother tried to give me.

These two were always up on all the top fashions at the time. As I get closer, I hear them talk about how dope the pea coat was and blah blah blah and now I am like "oh shit my mom was right it was a good coat". As I leave school and get back home, I asked my mother "what happened to the coat you were trying to give me"? She said, "I gave it away" I was like "what" and she said, "yea, I gave it away. I tried to tell you, but u kept saying you didn't want it". And there I stood looking like a damn idiot. I missed my ride on the cool kid fashion bus because I didn't listen to what she was trying to tell me. And that right there my friends is a cold case of the "you should have listened to me" blues you idiot.

Now, most people mean well, and they are trying to help you or do the right thing even though it may not seem like it to you at the time. Hell, a lot of kids may look at it as if this person is too old to understand me and they do not know what they are talking about. You got some kids that do not even believe these adults were once kids, what does this old fuddy duddy know about anything. Sheesh, respect your elders young girl and young man lol. Listen bro, some of these kids have a crazy way of perceiving things and that's because they only see things from their perspective. Hell, tv, cartoons, videogames and wrestling help shape their imaginations, but the smart ones listen eventually. It may take some time for logic and real comprehension to set in but maybe after a couple of hard lessons, some will listen, and some will get it. Personally, I just hope you get it in time, so you do not become like us. Trust me kid, we've been around these blocks more than you can imagine and hopefully at some point you'll be able to do the same thing and pass these ancient artifacts of knowledge on to other people that may need it.

Chapter 5

Kids Are Kids

Even though kids are extremely smart, kids are still kids. I think adults give kids too much credit at times. I say this because a kid may do something stupid and their parents might yell at them and say, "Boy, why you do that" and the kid goes "I don't know". Now, that parent is looking at it like why you didn't use common sense but sometimes kids do not have common sense and they are scared because they fear what the parent may do to them. As an adult we know if you add $1+1 = 2$, but I feel in a kid's mind at some point they think what if it could be something else Like $1+1 =$ apples, if you get what I'm saying lol. If you do not get my example, what I am trying to say is sometimes kids' imagination makes them believe things could be different than what they actually are, even if it's not logical. They may even feel like the adult is trying to trick them so that's why they don't fully believe them.

Some kids want to prove adults wrong because adults feel they must always be right and just for once they want to show them up. Kids believe in magic and fairy tales and to them your way is not right, mine is and we've all been there at some point. Your parents always think they know it all and most of the time they sort of do because they saw numerous situations or scenarios like this before playing out while the kid has not. Most kids are always looking to outsmart an adult and that's just the way it is. Kids often see things as a game and watching tv and YouTube may have contributed to this. How many times have you wanted to make your teachers look dumb in front of your friends so yawl could laugh at them? How many times have you wanted to be a smart ass or know it all and prove you were more superior? We have all been there, and kids are no different just on a smaller level and that is what the mentality of most kids. They do not know any better even though you told them. Kids can be very cunning, sometimes too arrogant but they are still trying to figure life out as they grow just like most adults.

Another thing is if you yell at a kid, they feel like they are going to get in trouble or possibly get hit so they freeze up. As a parent or older adult all they know is, I want an answer and you are taking too long, or you did not do this right after I told you what should have been done and that's the dilemma. There are 2 different perspectives of the same situation going on and the parents only see what they want, not really understanding the kid is traumatized at that moment. The typical kid is scared of backlash and the more you yell at them the more frightened and scared they become to respond or to do the right thing. Now, granted all kids are not like this and you got some downright bad asses who know just what they are doing but we cannot put all kids in the same category. Everyone reacts to things differently, but no one looks at it from both sides just their own. and that right there is the start of a lot of problems between kids and adults. Acting or parenting a certain way may now make your child afraid to talk to you because of their fear of backlash.

Granted, most parents are trying to establish law and order but the way the kid perceives it, they may now find it impossible to express themselves fully for fear of being yelled at or hit. With all this happening, they may now turn to a cool aunt, uncle, or big momma who's less like their parent and now when the parent notices this they become upset or why can't you talk to me not realizing they instilled to much fear into their own child when they were just really mirroring what was done to them when they were young. For some families, it's a vicious cycle and once again most adults are still trying to figure their own life out while trying to help the kids with theirs. It's a crazy situation but with love, patience, and good communication we can all get through it. Nobody in life is perfect, but we all make mistakes constantly and hopefully we are all striving to be better versions of ourselves but just like everything in life that takes time. We must forgive people when they fall short. It may be difficult at times but that is how we can all become closer as a family and a unit.

Also keep in mind, kids are going to lie because they think their parents are dumb enough to believe them and why you ask? Because they are kids that's why! Lol and they do not know any better. Your parents have been here way longer than you, duh! Television gives kids a crazy imagination and it convinces them that their schemes are going to work not knowing parents have done all their tricks 20 times over. So, they know when you are lying, plotting or up to something. Parents know your potential, but they do not know how their actions affect you psychologically. They mean well but it's a game that both parties are playing. Adults want to help kids grow up best as they can, and kids are fighting to find their way while trying to fit in this new world around them. We all are one in the same, but life is crazy and unexpected. You never know what is going to happen. Most people wake up not knowing whether this is their last day on earth or walking outside and the drunk driver was going to end their friend's life. It is just something no one knows so we are all just winging it.

I remember this one incident where I lied to my mom because I was a stupid kid if you will. So, one day I am home, and I wanted a haircut, but my mom didn't have the money at the time so like the genius I was in the 6th grade, I decided hey maybe I could cut my own hair. Hell, the barber did it, I saw him do it before, why couldn't I do the same thing right? Fuckin idiot lol. So, I take a pair of scissors and start cutting my hair and like a dummy, I put the hair under the couch because no one would think to look there right and I'd do such a good job just maybe I could start doing my own hair right? Wrong lol. Anyway, my mother comes home from work and sees my hair and asks me what happened, and I tell her I don't know. How stupid could I be right? So, she is walking around me looking at my head and she says, boy what happened to your hair and me being a kid I tell her it fell out. She says it fell out. I'm like yeah. Now, obviously I had no type of barber skills whatsoever so I can only assume I had patches all over my head. How good of a job could I have done?

In my mother's head, I know she was like "I know this ninja is lying and did it, but I want to hear the truth". So, she says it fell out? and I'm like yeah but on the couch, there laid the scissors and on the floor some of my hair that did not make it all the way under the couch. My mom sees this, puts 2 and 2 together and slaps my ass lol. Then she proceeds to take the scissors and begins to start cutting my hair even worse and says you want to lie to me and cut your own hair, now you're going to go to school with it like this. Once again, a kid thinks they can get away with stuff, they think they can outsmart their parents and tell them anything not knowing parents are smarter and they've been here longer but what do I know. Get it together please get it together bro.

Chapter 6

Stay positive

Always remember there is no expiration date on a dream. With that being said, I am going to tell you what someone told me a while ago. You do not have dreams, you have goals. Goals can be obtained once you write them down, focus on them, and work hard to achieve them. People may try to knock you or your vision down because they do not have goals for themselves. They do not want you to succeed because they never succeeded. They couldn't do the things they wanted to do, and it pains them to see you trying to do your thing, so they'll ask you why are you wasting your time? That will never work, you wasted all that money and got no results, and the negativity keeps pouring in. You cannot listen to any of that. Your goals only die when you decide to stop working to make them happen. Look at the most established stars or people who did big things with major companies, products, or movies. They all made it when they were older, and you know why? It's because they did not listen to the people who told them they were not going to make it. They followed their heart, mind, worked hard and stayed focused. Your goals can be accomplished at any age if you never give up on them.

Plenty of people will tell you, you're wasting your time and money but if you love what you are doing keep going for it. You have no clue how many people are stuck working jobs that they hate and dread coming to everyday. At least if you can do what you love doing, you will be a happier individual. There is no better feeling than doing what you always want to do and that's when it doesn't feel like work. And besides, you only have to be right one time so why not keep shooting for the stars. Most of the time with a lot of things, it's just being in the right place at the right time or coming across the right people to help you get things accomplished. You must always be ready and stay prepared. You never know when your opportunity is going to come. Life is crazy like that man. I do not know why it's set up like this but we're all just trying to play the hand we were dealt.

For example, I remember when I was heavy into making my music years ago, I used to always hear "always keep a demo on you because you never know who you'll meet". For those who do not know what a demo is, it's a snippet of your best songs on a cd but most of yawl don't even know what a cd or cassette tape is, anyway, so let me school you! See back in the day before YouTube, streaming, iPod, iPad, phones with music on it, me and all the other dinosaurs used to listen to music on these round discs that went into your car, stereo, or disk player and that's how we listened to music. Things have really changed from then to now, but I digress and back to the story. Anyway, always keep a demo on you, always keep a demo on you yea, yea, yea.

I used to hear that for years and I did it from time to time but not all the time. Lo and behold, one day I am visiting a friend who flew in from out of state and was staying at a hotel. As I got out of the cab right before I entered the hotel, I saw MS U.N.I.T.Y. Queen Latifah driving and stopping right in front of me. Now, I was in awe and shock because I would have never imagined I would see her face to face in a hotel parking lot. She spoke and told me to have a goodnight and right then and there it hit me. Had I been prepared and kept the demo on me like people told me for years I could have given her my cd and my path might have been different. Hell, I might not even be writing this book. I could have been a mega star chilling in a mansion with a haram full of women and people serving me like Mr. Belvedere but obviously that was not my path. I partially believed what they told me because nothing ever happened for years, so I say that to say this.

You must always be prepared because you never know when something is going to happen, and you may never get another shot like that again.

Also, always stay positive. Good energy attracts good energy, vibes, and people. Whatever type of energy you transmit is what you are going to receive back. If you think things are all bad, then that's what things are going to be. Your mind set and energy determines how your mood or day goes. Be thankful for what you have because a lot of people are way worse off compared to you and your problems. Someone always has it much worse than you do, and I don't think people stop to appreciate what they have or how far they've come a lot of times. Try to see the glass half full. Look at the brighter side of things with positive reinforcement and our world can be a better place.

It does not make a difference when you achieve your dream as long as you do. Remember there is no time limit. A lot of people feel if things do not happen for you when they say it will, it will never happen and that is totally false. Your timeline for things to happen are only for you not when someone else thinks it should be. Things are going to happen when they are supposed to no later or sooner than the creator wants them to happen. You also have to speak things into existence. Talk to the universe and be specific in what you want. You have to believe what you say. Your words are powerful, and you have to treat them as such. If you say you will do something, you will and if you think you will not, then you will not. Write down what you want and believe it. Remember you do not have dreams, you have goals. People work harder to make goals happen. Positivity, good planning, and a little bit of luck goes a long way.

Chapter 7

Take Chances

In life, you have to take chances especially early on. You need to do this because it makes you fearless and you never know what could happen. Something like this can either make or break you. Also, it lets you know what you are made of. The one time you tried and thought you were going to fail might lead to a new connection or outlook on things. A new ally, new method of looking at things you never thought was possible. Failed opportunities help you get closer to your goals because you now can see where you messed up, what missteps were taken, what things need to be tightened up or improved upon so next time you are better prepared. Better equipped to conquer your goals so you can eventually succeed the way you want to. Getting up, taking chances, performing in front of people or crowds takes a lot of guts and confidence and not everyone is built for that task.

Have you ever heard of the term practice makes perfect? That's exactly what it is. When someone plays sports, they have to practice day in and day out so they can make the team, become elite, and perform on a high level. That is what you are trying to do. Public speakers do not just wake up and become good they practice over and over again. They study, they know what they are talking about, they are well prepared so when it is time to deliver, nothing is going to break their concentration and methods because they know what to do. They are going to perform at an elite and professional level. It all started from them deciding to take a chance, a leap of faith, and if you will, by stepping out there and trying. Sometimes we are our own worst enemy. Fear can stop us from doing a lot of things. In our head, we create things that are not even there and that can be dangerous. We are too worried about what someone may think or say when really, we just need to go out and perform and leave it all out on the floor no matter what anyone thinks. As long as you know, you did your best it doesn't matter. Everyone has their own opinion. We are not going to let that affect us from doing what we got to do. Comprende amigo?

Back in my day of performing, early on it was exceedingly difficult. Most of the time, most people did not know you so when you were performing, a lot of people were not going to clap or cheer for you. Especially, if you were not part of their circle. They would just mostly look at you and stare. I remember at one of my very first open mics shows, we had 1-person clap after our performance, and it was a terrible site to behold lol. Now, we were not bad, it's just no one knew us and if you've ever been on a stage with nothing but people out in the crowd just staring at you it's a very scary site. If you were not strong enough, it could definitely make you never want to go back out there again but I took a different approach from that experience.

I realized what was going on and I decided in my mind it didn't make a difference how many people knew me. When I was out there, I was going to put on a show whether you knew me or not. I was going to make sure someone in the crowd was going to know I was there, and I did my thing. I would go in the crowd, stand on tables, get up in people's faces, physically take someone's hand and move it from side to side. Yea, I did all that shit. From that alone, people slowly started to give me my props, showing love, getting to know me and my crew. So, as we performed more and more, we were more accepted and recognized. It all came from taking a chance and learning what worked and what did not. It made me a better performer.

On a social tip dating wise, when you like someone whether male or female take a chance and ask them out. A lot of people spend too much time thinking about the fear of rejection. What if they say no, oh I'm going to die, I'm really feeling them, and they don't think I'm attractive as such and such. Get out of your feelings and head bro. Rejections are not as bad as you think. If someone rejects you, do not take it personal. They just literally prevented you from wasting your time and your time is unbelievably valuable. We as people build up unnecessary scenarios in our heads, making things more complicated than they really are. We are too worried about being embarrassed about what someone might say or think about us, in all actuality none of that stuff really matters. At least if you ask the person you can get your answer and know what it is and then ultimately try and find someone that wants you like you want them. Easier said than done though right?

Trust me bro, there are plenty of instances where people wanted to date someone, and they were too scared to say how they felt. When the guy finally digs up the nerve to ask the girl, she's now taken and then she says, "why didn't you say something sooner we could have worked on it and had something" or "I never knew you felt that way after all that time, why didn't you say something". Yep, you are going to hear stuff like that a lot when you wait too late. Ultimately, it turns into a missed opportunity that you can never really ever get back unless it's 4 or 5 years down the road. If you are lucky, take the chance sooner than later ninja. We have a million and one things running through our heads and most of the time, it is all over hyped and they never play out like we thought it would. It all depends on how much stock we put into our own emotions and how we think we're going to be viewed, but 9 out of 10 times, we as people always overreact.

Chapter 8

College Isn't for Everyone

Now, despite what your parents or teachers may tell you college is definitely not for everyone. Don't get me wrong, you are going to have a lot of fun but it's going to be some high-priced fun especially if you're not on a paid scholarship. In my personal opinion, you meet a lot of different people you would probably never come in contact with and you get your first real sense of grown up life. You live by yourself or share an apartment. No one's looking over your shoulder demanding you go to class. You can skip class anytime you want, play video games all day, go chill with women and guys on campus, go out and party any night of the week, and practically do any and everything you want. Sounds like a good life, right? The only problem with this is if you don't keep your grades up, you might lose your scholarship and your parents definitely aren't going for you wasting tons of their money because all you want to do is skip classes, party, and be an American idiot.

The truth is most people do not graduate college and get left with tons of debt they wind up paying back forever, forever ever, forever, ever. Even if you do graduate, most people do not get a job in the field they majored in. In my personal opinion, it's one big scam. Now, if you are going to be a doctor, nurse, lawyer, etc. Of course, you will get a good job but how much money was spent to become that profession? Most of the time, people have a hard time getting their dream job because 6 months after you graduate, you have to start paying back Salle Mae and whatever other group that helped set your ass up. You cannot get the job you want so you have to settle for whatever to make ends meet. Also, a lot of these businesses really give you the run around after you have graduated. Either they want you to work for free for a certain amount of years or you are too overqualified. It is one big mess if you ask me. But this goes back to you having the hook up, it's not what you know it's who you know. I will say if you do go to college, definitely make sure you intern for whatever job you want. That way if you do this, you are building a relationship in a company that may potentially hire you when you graduate. A lot of times your advisors are supposed to tell you this and help you with these things but like I said in most colleges they let you do what you want, it is your life. No one will twist your arm or babysit you. Your decisions are your decisions like a true adult. They might suggest things but never enforce them. If you listen, you listen if you don't, you don't. Hey, it is your parent's money you are wasting or the debt you are building up anyway right?

Most colleges and people do not care about you, they just want your money. They root for you to do good but really do not care. You are just another number bringing money to the school and government. The tuition is already high as hell and trust and believe it goes up every year, so you need to get in and get out. You cannot be wasting mommy and daddy's money because they are definitely struggling to make ends meet so you can have a "better future". Most of the classes you take will have nothing to do with your major so what's the true purpose of having it. You need to be focusing on the classes you really need and what you really want to do? That is one thing I never got about college. You spend money on books you'll only use once. When you sell it back, it's worth less than what you bought it for.

The school turns around and sells it to another student full price the following semester. Shame on you mutha cluckas! Nothing but highway robbery. Classes teach you unnecessary things, you will never use again and that is the nature of why it is such a big scam to me. The teachers don't really care if you pass or fail, it's your money you are wasting not theirs. Advisors let you do what you want so if you take the wrong classes you will be there an extra year. It's simply crazy like that but hey you're a young adult now so go out there and get them tiger!

These entities are literally lining you up so they can screw you over and possibly keep you in debt for most of or the rest of your adult life. Do not take it from me, ask around and see if I'm telling the truth. Yep, if you're lucky you might pass that debt along to your kids so they can continue the cycle. The flipside of college for me is, it's probably the last true time you actually get to be a kid or young adult. You get to have all the fun you want and meet new people. It's everything you can think of. Might I add, you can have sex, drugs, rock n roll all while your parents foot the bill. You'll have a great time, but just so you know, the real world is waiting right around the corner for you with a brick in its hand and next thing you know pow! Yep, I told you so. After high school trust and believe it's a crazy world out there ready to devour any and everybody up with no remorse buddy.

For me personally, I told my daughter she is not going to college. I told her she's going to the job corps. Now, most people would be like why send her there? My response is that the job corps is better than college. They let you stay on campus for free, teach you a trade for whatever you want to do, they find you a job when you graduate, and they pay you while you're in school training. You definitely cannot beat that. Why let my daughter get trapped into a bunch of debt by a system that is just going to screw her over in the long run? Not on my watch bucko. If you are going to go to college, at least look at the world and see what is the direction of things so that way, you can major in something the world would need like computer tech or some type of repair, doctor, lawyer, therapist things of that nature until the robots take over but that's another story for a different day. The world needs people who can do things like that. I feel a lot of parents want to push their kids to do better than them and a lot of them may not have had the opportunity to go to or finish college so naturally they push their kids not knowing the long-term effects of debt that lie ahead. Once again these are my opinions, you do not have to listen to me. I am just merely giving suggestions to help provide options on your journey. A lot of things I say, trust me no one's going to give it to you like this and if they did you still might not listen.

Chapter 9

Mind Your Own Business

Simple and plain sometimes you may want to help out, but you have got to mind your own damn business. I know you mean well, and most people want to do good, but the simple fact of the matter is no one is asking you for your 2 cents (go figure and here I am giving you mine smh lol). Most times, people do not really need help, some want to just use you and direct your attention to them. When deciding to help out, you may do more harm and damage than you expect. You heard the phrase don't save her because she doesn't want to be saved. A lot of people cry wolf and a lot of people like being in the situation they are in. This does not apply to everyone but in my opinion, don't do it to yourself and let that person or party figure it out.

First example, I remember someone told me that my friend 's boyfriend was cheating on her and with that being said, I had 2 options. I could either tell her or mind my damn business. On one end, if I told her, it would mean she could confront the guy. They would get into a back and forth and could possibly break up, right? Everyone wants to help their friend and people out if you can, but hold on bro, here is the flipside to that. On the other end, what if she spoke to him and he twisted the whole situation around and they stayed together anyway. He could tell her that I was trying to break them up because I wanted to be with her. She could possibly believe him, and it would make our friendship awkward because she was trying to work it out with him. He could then say distance yourself from your friend so they could work things out. It could just turn into a total mind fuck and no one wants an unnecessary headache. On that note, I decided to butt out and let her find things out on her own. They eventually broke up. I definitely did not want to get involved with a he said, she said situation. It is always best to stay out of other people's situations and relationships because adding information whether true or false, could always make unnecessary problems for both parties. What if the information I had received was wrong? What if someone were trying to break them up, by me giving bad information? It could help propel someone else's lies or agenda. There is an old saying that out of sight out of mind or what you do not know will not hurt you. If you do not know about something, you will not think about it. Sometimes people need to let things play out and handle things on their own. What is done in the dark, eventually comes to the light at some point.

Example number 2, my cousin's baby father went out to a club with his friend to go let off some steam. Within the party, there was a fight that broke out and the baby father's friend broke it up. He did not know either party, but he was trying to be a good guy. They assumed everything was ok and they continued to have a good time. Once the party was over, they exited the club and to everyone's surprise one of the guys that were fighting, came back with a gun and shot and killed the baby father's friend. He did not even know the guys and was trying to do a good thing but in the process, it costed him his life. You do not know people's mind set, you do not know if they are on drugs, out for revenge or whatever the case is. Obviously, this killer did not care about anything. All he knew was, he wanted revenge on a guy that did not mind his own business. He wanted revenge on a guy that prevented him from handling his business on someone. It was a sad outcome the way it played out. No one knows what day will be their last. Just try to do the best you can and mind your own damn business.

Last example, I remembered when I was in high school, my best friend and I were walking, and we saw a couple that was in a heated argument. The guy was literally yelling and whooping the woman's ass in the street. I really felt bad for this woman and I wanted to help her. Many times, you feel bad for someone who's being abused and want to do something about the situation happening in front of you. What if that was my mom, sister, or aunt? What if I could save them from embarrassment and harm? As we walked by and witnessed this, I said to my friend "let's go and help her, we can take him". When I started to go over there, he grabbed my arm and said, "mind your damn business". I said, "but she needs our help" and his reply was "what if he has a weapon on him and he hurts or kills one of us"? What if we whoop his ass and she still stays with him? What if when they get home, he kills her because he thinks she set him up by having us come there? We can make this situation a lot worse by interfering. You do not know what she did to make this guy do what he is doing. Never get into anyone's personal problems, especially someone you do not know. Let them figure that shit out. If she wants to get out of that situation let her. She can leave, get some family members to help, or call the cops. My boy was absolutely right. In that instance, a multitude of things could have happened and could have gone wrong. Things are never what they appear to be especially if you do not have all the facts. So, do yourself a favor and mind your own damn business.

Chapter 10

Peer pressure is a Mutha

Now, growing up is tough especially when you hit high school. You might start feeling outside pressure from friends or people who you thought were friends who will probably leave you high and dry when the shit hits the fan. Trust me, everyone you think is a friend is definitely not, but you will learn soon enough. Oftentimes most people only end up with maybe 2 (if they're lucky) best friends in their life when everything is said and done. Most times your parents can spot things in a person you cannot, and you know why? Because they have been there before. They see it all and most times they can tell by the way people act. A good parent is good at looking at certain signs and reading people so if your parents tell you something about someone, listen to what they are saying. Also, your teachers are pushing you harder by giving you more work, students coming at you sideways, possible bullies picking on you, and just life in general is coming at you in full force. On that note, welcome to the world of high school bro. Everyone wants to be a rebel. Everyone does not want to be looked at as smart or a geek. People are calling you names, trying to start fights, lying on you, all types of shit but you got to stay cool and positive. It's not the end of the world if things do not work out how you planned, it's a work in progress, just like you.

I'm sure you are going to want to be a part of the cool kids, the in crowd if you will and who would not? No one wants to be looked at like an oddball (see Napoleon and Steve Urkel) trust me. You got to have the newest clothes, the best sneakers, and the best shoes. You have also got to have your hair done, fresh cut and unfortunately mom and dad may not be able to make it happen all the time because the funds are tight, so you better get ready for a rough year. You better learn how to come back with some jokes to silence those critics coming at your neck. A long supply of infinite disses will make life a whole lot easier for you, trust me, but this is where things start to shift. In the grand scheme of things, all that stuff is materialistic. We all like nice things but ultimately it does not matter. School is a big fashion show, and you think everyone's opinion matters but it actually does not. Most of those people, you will probably never see again once you graduate. A lot of times in your mind the things you thought were dyer or so critical at that time, it really was not. In our mind, sometimes we make things more important than they really are.

Your parents told you certain things to look out for and they're trying to save you whether you think they are too strict or not. They know all too well about wrong decisions that can get your life sidetracked. Having unprotected sex can get you a baby to quick, hanging with the wrong crowd can get you thrown in jail, or a record at an early age and sometimes it could lead to yours or someone else's death. Your friends might try and convince you to start drinking and smoking and yea it looks cool but long term you are headed for some serious addiction and health problems. Everyone wants to look, and act grown and have fun, but you will pay the price sooner or later. Whether it's cutting school to go see a guy or girl, showing up at the party smoking cigarettes or weed, it is going to set you up for a check your body can't cash. Smoking and drinking at an early age can definitely turn your insides into a total mess. Long term effects that you do not see now but when you are older it will definitely give you complications that will keep you on medicines and in and out the hospital. You may try to resist but oftentimes it is not as easy but the best thing to do is try and remove yourself from tempting situations like that. Your future self will definitely thank you, but what do I know?

Chapter 11

Family Ties

Now, just because yawl family don't mean shit. Yea that is your cousin, that is your sister, brother, uncle or whoever. Yea, yea, I know but that doesn't mean shit. People will do you wrong but not like your family. Not all family is bad but boy let me tell you, some of them muthas are only out for themselves. You also have some that steal from you and some that all they do is lie so you cannot believe shit they say. Some get drunk and can't hold their liquor and some that decide I'm not messing with none of yawl so you not going to see me unless it's a family reunion and even then, you not going to see me for long. Lend someone some money and they think they don't have to pay you back. You're going to fight, you're going to argue, and yes that's family but you got some individuals that will do you dirty with no remorse and think that everything is alright. You know people got selective memories, man. Like, you should not have a problem with them fucking you over. Sometimes your friends are more family than your own family. That blood is thicker than water shit, it's only right sometimes man let me tell you.

Example number one, my mother moves away to South Carolina and leaves me and my 2 cousins the apartment to be adults and live our life. We are supposed to cover all the bills and do what we have to do to survive. We all go to work every day but when it comes to the bills, they do not give me everything they owe. I get a ton of excuses on how they will give it back to me the following week, how they got short on their check, I put their part up for them and they will pay me back yada, yada. One thing my mother always told me was to handle your bills. She said the landlord does not care about anything but that rent so whatever you have to do, sacrifice, and pay those bills. Anything you may want needs to come after you take care of the bills first. This was my whole outlook, but my cousins did not see things the way I did. Lo and behold I find out they were just holding on to their money and spending it. Doing whatever they wanted to do because the bills were not in their name. They were treating people to restaurants, buying clothes doing all types of dumb shit instead of handling their business. So, here I am trying to keep a roof over our heads, putting out all my money, borrowing off credit cards, trying to make ends meet and they are not even considering anything but their own well-being. See that is the bullshit right there. After a few months I moved out and left them high and dry and they had the nerve to wonder why? Man get the fuck out of here, right.

Example number two, sometimes we just do not learn from the first time around. I moved into an apartment with my credit fucked up because of my punk ass no good cousins. I am trying to recover and get back on the right track. One of my cousins called me and said they were in a jam and have nowhere to go and needed a place to stay and things will not be like it was before. Feeling bad for them, I get it approved so they can stay with me and my roommate and everything starts out fine at first. Before you know it, they lose their job because they really do not want to work. They would rather stay home, collect unemployment, and play videogames all day long. Now, they are always short or late with the rent. I'm slowly getting back to the same situation I was in before. At one point, I tried to help them by selling them an old car I had for dirt cheap. Then they still acted like I was the problem. They had an attitude with me like I did something wrong. Sometimes man people fuck you over with no regard. A lot of times, people think you are obligated to help them all the time or feel sorry for them but what about you? Even though you are family that does not mean anything, man. Right is right wrong is wrong. They completely ignore or forget how they screwed you over or put you in a bind. Also, they never apologize or try to make up for it. If they do try to pay you back, they will never pay you the full amount of what they owe. At the end of the day, most jokers do not care and some not all, but some people are just lazy and selfish.

In a lot of cases, that one guy who is like a brother or girl who is like a sister will do more for you than anyone else and that right there is family. Family is not just the people you are related to, it's the people that will be there for you and help you out no matter what. Family can be the one you can call to talk to, the one that will never judge you, and the one who will be there and be down for you no matter what. When you get older, you will realize most of the time, most people don't even hang out with their family or certain members like that anyway all because of things that might have happened way back, but hey man that's life. Life is a funny thing because you never know how things will turn out. You may experience things that you would have never thought would happen in a million years, but it does. People will turn their back on you and betray you but hopefully you will have someone in your corner to ride with you when no one else will.

Chapter 12

Credit Cards

Do yourself a favor and watch out for those damn credit cards, man. They try to get you while you're young, and it is a set up. You may get them in the mail thinking you can buy this or that, and you do not have to worry about it because you will pay for it later and that's exactly how they get you. They hit you with a crazy interest rate. Plus, you're young, why the hell should you read the fine print that shows you exactly how they're going to bend you over and screw you with no Vaseline, right? That my friend is why they do it. They know most people, especially kids, are not paying attention to all that. You definitely are not reading all that small fine print. You're going to buy what you want, forget to pay it, or shrug it off like it's nothing and they're going to tack on late fees interest rates and before you know it that $50 purchase is going to turn into $200 or more later on. Do not do it, trust me these bastards will come for you sooner or later.

I remembered me getting my first credit card and what did my mother tell me? Boy, cut that card up, throw it away, do not use it, they're going to screw you over and you're not going to pay them back and what did I do in true young adult fashion? I ignored my mom and figured I could prove her wrong. I could be responsible and handle my business. I activated the card, brought what I wanted, and did not make payments like an idiot and the late fees and interest piled up. What she said was exactly what happened. I did not pay it, got hit with crazy fees making it almost four times the amount I spent. After numerous calls and letters from the bank, they gave it to a debt collector, and they hounded me constantly and then they contacted my job to take the money out of my check every week. Then they tried to get double slick because after I paid them off, they tried to collect the same debt twice. As a kid, we do things not knowing how to handle the situation thinking we could figure it out and handle it on our own and that is how we get fucked up. These companies are banking on you fucking up so they can put you into a trap. Be smarter than me and a lot of other people who thought they were getting some shit for free with no consequences. Do not fall for the leaves over the hole, bro stay awake.

Credit cards are not all bad, it's just the decision we make with them. You can actually do a lot of good with them, It's just we have to get the right guidance and maturity to do so. With the right people around to guide us, we can always have a better outcome. Hey man, no one's perfect, we all make mistakes, and we are going to keep making them until we die. We just hope we can get better with time and learn from past experiences. A lot of people want to help you avoid the pitfalls they fell into. We want you to be a better version of us, a better version of yourself and if I can get you to a better way of life, it is fine by me. Excellence is what we are striving for and you have to have goals and positivity going forward. Stick with me kid, knowledge and positivity reinforcement can go a long way.

Chapter 13

Learn How to Read People

Moving forward you have to learn how to figure people out. You have to be a good judge of character. This will definitely help you see people's intent. Like, I told you before not everyone is your friend. It is a lot of people who hang with you all the time and talk about you like you are nothing behind your back. Some people will smile in your face and hate your guts. Some people want nothing but to bring you down because they are jealous of you. They cannot stand that you are doing something better than them. You look better, dress better, play sports better, get more girls or guys better and in the words of the famous Tupac song, "that's just the way it is". These people have their own insecurities, but it is up to you to pick up on the signs before you become a casualty of their cruelty. Before you get betrayed or backstabbed, do not put anything past anyone. These people are dangerous, so you have to constantly be aware.

I remembered when I was in high school, I was dating this chick named Monique. I would go over her house after school to chill but as time went on, I noticed one of my classmates started dating her sister. My classmate played basketball and he had an exchange student named Harrold living with him who also played basketball. I would speak to them from time to time and say what's up on school grounds. The vibe was always cool, we had no problems with each other. I knew both of them, but we were not really friend friends like that. As time went on, one day Monique and I got into a huge argument because she heard that I was dating another chick which was a total lie. We got into it really bad and we broke up. Fast forward a few years later, I ran into her and we began talking. I asked her why she believed that lie. I told her it was all a lie and I never cheated on her. I asked her who told her all that and she told me it was the kid Harrold and then it all made sense. Harrold knew I was dating her, and he wanted in. Since my classmate dated the sister, if he lied on me, he could date Monique and they all could chill together with me out the way and that is what happened. Yea, he was cordial in my face and kept it cool but the whole time he was plotting, that's how people are. If someone sees something they want, oftentimes they will do whatever it takes to get it even if that means lying on you and that's reality.

Another time I remembered I was dating this girl. Me, her, and her girlfriend Monica used to always talk on the phone all hours of the night all the time, just us three. Watching tv shows together and just talking about any and everything. As time went on, me and my girlfriend started to have problems, disagreements whatever you want to call it. I would ask Monica what could I do to make things right between me and her. She would give me advice, but things never seemed to get better. At one point I asked Monica to talk to her since it did not seem like my girlfriend was listening to me and to this day, I will never forget what she told me. She said I'm not doing that, I said why not, and she said because I'm her friend not yours. That was one of the biggest verbal slaps in the face I ever received. That showed me the whole time I thought we were friends it was all an illusion. I was talking to the enemy the whole time and did not even realize it. She straight played me, and I never even saw it. Oftentimes your perception and people's perception are two totally different things. You think it's one way and it's totally something else.

As time moved forward, I began to look at people's actions and reactions to certain things. I asked questions, listened to their responses, things of that nature and I have gotten better over time. Within the first few minutes, I can usually tell how someone is by nine times out of ten and I am usually right. I go off vibes and energies. Not everyone can do that, but it is a true gift. Trying to do things of that nature will help you figure out who needs to be around you and who should not. Always pay attention to your surroundings because you never know who wants to do bad things to you. You could prevent someone from trying to attack you, rob you or hurt you. These dangers are all around and if we do not pay attention we could get hurt.

In my youth, I used to walk through all bad neighborhoods like a dummy. I did it not because I was tough but because nothing ever happened to me. I always assumed nothing would happen because I did it for so long. Rough blocks, jokers on the corners, just some of the worst areas possible but my ignorance caught up with me one day. This particular night I was going back to college and the bus was taking too long so I had nothing but time on my hand. I decided to walk with my headphones on to waste time. As I began walking and listening to my music, a guy started walking on the side of me. I noticed him but did not really pay it no mind. At some point the guy cuts me off and says give me your money and now I am like o hell no let us fight. Yea, I could fight him but what I did not notice was he had at least 10 guys with him. They were all taller than me and now here I am surrounded. I was so into my music and not paying attention to what was going on or who was around me that they got the drop on me.

Nothing like this ever happened to me and now here I am in a situation. They searched my pockets and did not find anything. I had my money hidden and I kept telling the dude I didn't have anything. One of the guys said let him go, he doesn't have nothing man and I say yea man I don't have nothing let me go. In that instance, he finds the money and I am like oh shit. Now, if you from the hood like me you know criminals and hoodlums do not like to be lied to and from here on out it's only going to get worse. I already knew I was most likely going to get jumped. So, I tell the dude come on man let me go, you already got my money man and then he says what you say? He half turns and before you know it POW! I got hit in the face with the guy's fist. I do not know what he had in his hand, but it definitely cut my face. The impact of the punch, I fell back into a gate and with the momentum from that, I pushed through the crowd and began to run. They chased me for a little bit, but I got away. Now, I have no problem fighting but eleven against one is definitely not good odds. All I knew was I had to get out of there because all it could take is for someone to hold me down while everyone attacks me or stomp me, and I surely am no fool sir. Some may look at that situation as bad but for me, I am glad it happened. That was the lesson I needed. The incident alone made me wake up and pay attention to everyone and everything. In the streets and in life, most people only think about attacking you when you are not paying attention. Most times, if they see you are aware and know that you see what they are doing they will not try you.

Chapter 14

Believe in Yourself

Last but not least believe in yourself man. Words are powerful. Life and death are in the power of your tongue. Depending on what you say, it can and will come true if that is what you honestly believe in your heart. The universe is always listening whether you believe it or not. Sticks and stones break bones and words definitely do hurt in this day and age. If you want things to work out for you, work hard and go get them. Envision everything you say you want. Imagine that future, that car, that career. If you can see it, you can make it happen. Nothing is given to you, everything is earned. But if you speak and live on negative vibes, you are always going to have negativity around you. If you speak positively, you are always going to get positive results. A lot of people are miserable, and they try to put that on you. Do yourself a favor and don't let them. We all control our own destiny by what we do and do not do. There is a quote that says the very road a man tried to avoid is the same road where he finds his destiny. So, there is always a plan and purpose for things. We just do not see it until it happens.

On another note, you have to learn to count on yourself to make things happen. Oftentimes you will be disappointed waiting around for people to come help you. Not everyone wants to let you down but there are a lot of circumstances and moving parts that may prevent people from doing what they said they were going to do. Everyone is not genuine but that's life. Things work out when it's supposed to not when you want them too. Now, If you ask me to give you $100 dollars because you really need it and I say yea I got you but if they mess my check up or some emergency happens to where I can't do it unfortunately that's how things work sometimes and you can't get mad. I had every intent to help you out, but things didn't come through on my end. It is what it is sometimes. A lot of people feel if they depend on themselves, they will not be let down because at the end of the day, they can only blame themselves if they did not make the necessary steps to move forward. It's good to count on you. It is good to push yourself because at the end of the day in actuality, you are really competing with yourself. You are trying to become a better you every day. If you do not believe and invest in yourself, who will? You have to have confidence and fearlessness. If you don't succeed, try, try again. Rome was not built in a day. As long as you never give up, you will reach your destination.

Special Dedication

This book is dedicated to each and every young person and adult trying to find their way in this thing we call life. I realized growing up, a lot of people do not really have someone in their corner they can truly relate to that can properly guide and help them transition into adulthood and a better life. There are a lot of steps and missing conversations that fall through the cracks along the way. We may have our parents, family, friends, and others but as a kid during that crucial time, you do not know how to fully process things and handle them. It's always been, do what your parents say because they are right but as a kid most of the time they have doubts on what they're being told. Adults tell you things and you're stuck in a mental tug of war of what your parents say, what your friends or teachers say, what you see on tv, and hear on the radio. But things come down to how you really feel and what you see. A lot of times kids may get the "do what I say not as I do" from a parent but like I previously stated, the kid is trying to figure out life most of the time but so are the adults. Everybody is just trying to keep it together, trying to be happy, find happiness and make ends meet and still deal with the pressure and complications of life. We all learn by trial and error and we take bits and pieces of advice along the way.

In writing this book, I hope that I have shed some light for both adults and young people that have made the gap between us all a little bit smaller. Thank you for your support and I pray you can use some of these ancient artifacts in your life. Be blessed.

Made in the USA
Middletown, DE
24 November 2020

25139548R00046